Delhi Agra & Jaipur
The Glorious Cities

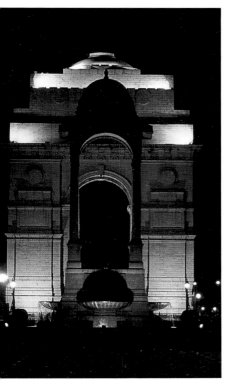

D1638626

Rupinder Khullar • Reeta Khullar

The Qutb Minar is a prestigious landmark of Delhi.

DELHI

Delhi is the capital of India and an ancient city steeped in history. Agra is a region symbolizing Mughal splendor and Jaipur is a land of colour and pageantry. These three cities, so diverse yet interlinked, because of their rich cultural and historical traditions, provide a glimpse into the true essence of India.

Delhi brings to mind a kaleidoscope of contrasting images which transport you back and forth in time. An intriguing synthesis of both the old and the new, Delhi, while embracing modernity has also preserved its glorious past.

No other city in India can boast of such an ancient, turbulent and heterogeneous history as perhaps Delhi. A study of the last 3,000 years reveals the rise and fall of many great empires here.

The origin of Delhi lies deeply embedded in its ancientness, the most plausible and convincing belief regarding the birth of this imperial city suggests that Delhi was mentioned in the epic Mahabharata as a capital of the Pandavas, a beautiful city named Indraprastha on the very site where ruins of Purana Qila now exists. Archaeological findings unearthed in this area are similar to those discovered in places associated with the Mahabharata, like the Kurukshetra. Evidence suggests that Delhi was continuously inhabited and fell prey to the mercenary designs of foreign invaders and conquerors because of its wealth and strategic position.

The history of Delhi is the history of its seven medieval cities. It is said that the name 'Delhi' was coined by the Rajputs who became prominent sometime in the late 7th century AD or early 8th century AD. Surajpal and Anangpal, the two Rajput chieftains of the Tomar clan, built an amphitheatre and a reservoir in the Surajkund area of the Aravalli ranges (now in Haryana) and the citadel of Lalkot in 1020 AD, where the Qutb Minar now stands. This was the first medieval city of Delhi.

A rival Rajput clan took possession of the city about a century later and Prithviraj Chauhan, extended the city's boundaries and called it Qila Rai Pithora, the ruins of which can still be seen in the Mehrauli area. The brave and chivalrous Prithviraj, was unfortunately, also the last Hindu king of Delhi. A sad betrayal by his own trusted chief Jai Chand led to his defeat at the hands of Mohammed Ghori in the battle of Tarain in 1192, thus bringing to an end of an important era in Indian history.

Qutbuddin Aibek, the trusted commander of Ghori, who rose to the position of a governor from a mere slave, assumed power as the first Sultan of Delhi after his master's death in 1206 and founded the Slave dynasty. This paved the way for the Muslim rule in India that would last almost 600 years. Aibek began destroying temples built by the Rajputs and also tried to change people's lifestyle. He laid the foundation of the Qutb Minar in 1209, the tallest tower in India, which was completed by his son-in-law Iltutmish after his death. Razia Sultan, Iltutmish's daughter, distinguished herself as the first woman ruler of Delhi when her father died. But her reign was short as the conservatives were against her.

Taking advantage of the prevailing disorder, Jalaluddin Khilji, an Afghan Turk, founded the Khilji dynasty in 1290, but was murdered by his nephew Alauddin Khilji. An avid builder, he created Siri, the second medieval city in 1303 AD, to the north of Qila Rai Pithora near the present day Hauz Khas and the Asiad Village Complex. His well-planned city had walls made of stone, brick and lime and a huge reservoir, Hauzi Alai.

Ghiyasuddin Tughlaq, set up Tughlaqabad, the third ancient city of Delhi in 1321 AD when he assumed power after routing the Khiljis. Situated eight km south east of Qutb Minar, this simple and spartan city, fortified with unusually thick walls made from rubble and plaster instead of the commonly used red sandstone were punctuated with bastions, gates and windows. Comprising a citadel, and a palace, its fragmented ruins today tell the tales of a city which was more a military stronghold than a metropolis.

Above: The ruins of Hauz Khas, the second city of Delhi.
Middle: The Quwwat-ul-Islam mosque in the Qutb Minar complex.
Top: An illuminated Qutb Minar.

Above: Inlay work on a wall inside the Red Fort.
Middle: Tughlaqabad as it appears today.
Top: A closeup of Humayun's tomb.

Mohammed Bin Tughlaq adorned the mantle of the next king when his father died in an unusual accident. This brought into existence Jahanpanah in 1325 AD, the fourth city of Delhi.

Lying amidst Qila Rai Pithora and Siri, this walled city also bore the austere Tughlaq style. Mohammad Bin Tughlaq's desire to extend his empire to Deccan, made him shift his capital along with its inhabitants to Devagiri in Maharashtra and rename Daulatabad. His plans went awry and within a decade he reverted back to Delhi with his people. Feroz Shah Tughlaq succeeded his cousin after his demise in 1351 AD. A distinguished ruler with a multifaceted persona of a scholar, architect and philanthropist, he set about improving the lot of his people and restored the glory of some of the old monuments of Delhi like the Qutb Minar and some structures at Suraj Kund. He also realized his ambition of creating Ferozabad, the fifty city of Delhi.

Built on a fertile piece of land extending from Hauz Khas to Kotla Feroz Shah on the banks of the river Yamuna, this beautiful city had lovely palaces, gardens, forts, mosques and towns which were later ravaged by Sher Shah Suri.

Delhi lost everything except its name when calamity struck in the form of Timurlane of Samarkand, who plundered and massacred the city and its people for a fortnight in 1398. Though the Tughlaqs continued to rule through the turbulence till 1413 AD, was the rule of Sayyids which brought some respite to the people. Ultimately it was the Lodis who tried to restore the prestige of the city they took over in 1450 AD. Sikander Lodhi shifted to Agra because of constant skirmishes with the Mongols but the first battle of Panipat proved disastrous for the next Sultan Ibrabim Lodi in 1526 when he lost both his life and his kingdom to Babur, a descendant of Timur, who became the first emperor of the Mughal dynasty in India. Agra remained Babur's capital during his brief rule of four years, but his eldest son Humayun chose to govern from Delhi after his father's death in 1530. He built a new city at the old fort named Dinapanah, which was also the location of the Pandavas of the Mahabharata. Humayun's reign of a decade was cut short when Sher Shah Suri, a trusted general of Ibrahim Lodhi defeated him.

Proving to be a very efficient ruler, Sher Shah Suri strengthened and extended both his empire and the Dinpanah city and renamed it Shergarh. These constituted the sixth ancient city of Delhi. After a 15 year exile, Humayun was able to recapture his throne from Sher Shah Suri's nephew. But, destiny willed otherwise. Humayun had ruled only for about a year during his second phase when he met with an accident and died.

In 1556, his 13 year-old son Akbar became the third Mughal monarch of India. A contemporary of Queen Elizabeth I, he is considered the most distinguished of all the kings of his dynasty. His endearing qualities included a tolerant attitude towards Hinduism and other religions and benevolence towards all. During his long and efficient rule of half a century, Delhi remained his capital for only eight years, as he decided to govern from Agra and Fatehpur Sikri.

Delhi remained a provincial city for both him and his son Jahangir. It was his grandson Shah Jahan who was ultimately responsible for restoring the imperial glory of Delhi. Shah Jahan ruled over his vast empire from Agra for about 11 years, but after the death of his wife Mumtaz Mahal and building of the wondrous monument – Taj Mahal in her memory, he moved to a new capital, Shahjahanbad, also known as the seventh ancient city of Delhi. The walled city with Red Fort as its citadel had the river Yamuna as its backdrop. It covered an area from present day Kashmiri Gate to Delhi Gate and had 14 imposing doorways, out of which, only five have survived. The majestic city had beautiful palaces, forts, mosques, gardens, houses and *bazaars*. Jama Masjid, the largest mosque in India, was also constructed by him and also Chandni Chowk or the Silver Street which was the heart of the city and a historic thoroughfare.

Though crowded and congested, Chandni Chowk retains its mediaeval charm even today. A visit to this momentous city also known as Old Delhi takes you back a few 100 ears to imagine if not experience the splendor and affluence of those times.

Aurangzeb imprisoned his father Shah Jahan and became the next Mughal monarch. hough he reigned for a long period, his austere and authoritarian ways made him npopular among his people. After his death in 1707, the indomitable Mughal dynasty egan to weaken and disintegrate. Nadir Shah invaded Delhi in 1739 and brutally utchered and bruised the city, stripping it of its immense wealth and treasures which included the famous Peacock Throne and the Kohinoor Diamond belonging to Shah han.

Ahmed Shah Durrani, a close associate of Nadir Shah, also struck in 1757, to take way whatever little was left in the city.

Delhi was in a state of total disarray and confusion following these two invasions. he weakened Mughals were desperately trying to maintain their control by thwarting ie attempts of the Marathas, Abdali and the Rohillas of Afghanistan to gain access to ie throne.

The East India Company which had come to India as traders had, meanwhile, eveloped political inclinations. Taking advantage of the crumbling Mughal empire and the onstant infighting among the smaller states, they defeated the Marathas and established dministrative control over Delhi while Calcutta remained their capital.

The last Mughal ruler Bahadur Shah Zafar was dethroned and sent to Burma and ie sun finally set on the fortunes of the Mughal dynasty.

Delhi remained an active participant during the revolt of 1857 or the First War of dian Independence but the British overpowered them. The accession of Edward VII the throne of England in 1903 was celebrated at a grand *durbar* followed by another ne in 1911, where George V announced that British architects, Sir Edwin Lutyens and r Herbert Baker, were to be assigned the project of building the new capital. Raisina ill was chosen as the pivotal point for the Viceregal Lodge, now known as Rashtrapati havan, around which the other important administration centres had to be built. New elhi was declared as the formal capital of the British India Empire in January 1931 id this was the eighth city of Delhi. Its fortunes again soared when New Delhi was tained as the capital of independent India.

Beginning from the Indus Valley Civilisation, building and architecture in India is been a dynamic process largely influenced by history, religion and climate. Delhi's recious monumental heritage is also interlinked with its distinguished history; the udy of one giving an insight into the other. The 1,300 listed monuments of Delhi's ncient and modern cities now in varying degrees of preservation, reflect each phase of do-Islamic architecture. All that remains of the city of Lalkot and Qila Rai Pithora are uins of the first defensive wall and some broken structures in Surajkund and Aanagpur im. The 4th century Iron Pillar (a metallurgical wonder with Sanskrit inscriptions) that is remained rust and corrosion free till today, was brought by Anang Pal and installed a Vishnu Temple which later became the site of Quwwat-ul-Islam mosque built by utbuddin Aibek. He mercilessly pulled down all Hindu and Jain temples and used the aterial for his construction work. This mosque was the first in northern India and had lot of Hindu ornamentations like tasselled ropes, bells, flowers and sculptures on its lars and corridors.

Qutbuddin built Qutb Minar, a prestigious landmark of Delhi, to proclaim the victory Islam in India and also for offering prayers. The five-storeyed red sandstone tower ith rounded angular flutings and exquisite brackets is richly carved with inscriptions. was completed by Iltutmish who also built a tomb for himself outside the Quwwat--Islam mosque, which is a beautiful example of the fusion of Hindu art with Islamic esign. The Akai Darwaza in red sandstone and marble was built by Alauddin Khilji in 311 as a southern gateway to the mosque. It is the first structure to follow complete lamic principals and an architectural marvel because of its harmonious proportions,

Above: The impressive Secretariat buildings lie on either side of Rajpath.
Middle: Sir Edwin Lutyen, the architect of the British Indian capital, New Delhi.
Top: The Rashtrapati Bhavan, is the official residence of the President of India.

The spectacular Republic Day celebrations held on 26th January every year commence from the Rajpath and end at the Red Fort.

perforated screen windows and horse-shoe-shaped arches. Among the scattered ruins of his once prosperous and flourishing city of Siri is the famous Hauz-i-Alai Tank with its stone steps.

The Tughlaq Dynasty founded three cities in a period spanning less than 300 years. Ghiyas-ud-Din's mausoleum along with the Fort of Adilabad, the Begumpuri Mosque and the Satpula of Jahanpanah city have distinguishing features like extraordinary thick and sloping walls and use of solid rubble and plaster in place of sandstone for strength and solidity. The city of Ferozabad exists only in the ruins of Feroz Shah Kotla adjoining a sports stadium. It consists of royal palaces, a mosque and a famous third century B.C. Ashokan Pillar brought by Feroz Shah from Punjab.

After the bloody carnage unleashed by Timurlane, the Sayyids had little time to devote to new constructions. So, the few monuments they built are simple and devoid of intricate ornamentation and other embellishments. The tomb of Mohammed Shah Sayyid in the Lodi Gardens is a large octagonal structure with massive arcades, pavilions and a large central dome. The Bada Gumbad has a mosque decorated not with carvings but inscriptions and foliage designs in plaster. The blue-glazed tiles in the interior of Sheesh Gumbad give it a glass-like appearance. The Lodis too did not use red sandstone or expensive marble and their grey granite tombs were small but sturdy and set the trend for the early garden tomb. The tomb of Sikandar Lodi arouses interest because of its unusual styled dome in different coloured tiles.

The architectural wealth of the Sultanate period reveals a mingling of Hindu and Islamic cultures which finally achieved a perfect synthesis in the later Mughal period. While the Indian mason was proficient in constructing huge stone temples decorated with carved panels, the Muslims brought in concepts of domes, minarets and arches from their mosques. There was one prolific builder in each dynasty and while the early capitals lay in the close vicinity of the rocky Aravallis, the later kings, having consolidated their empires, gradually moved towards more open spaces on the banks of the river Yamuna. Emperor Humayun's city, Dinapanah, is a prime example. He built an oblong shaped Purana Qila or Old Fort as a sturdy citadel with an unusually bold and spartan veneer. The buildings inside the fort like the Sher Mandal were constructed by Sher Shah Suri for his capital Shergarh. Humayun's Tomb situated to the south of Old Fort and near the holy pilgrim centre Nizamuddin Auliya is a fabulous structure built by his wife Haji Begum. The colossal red-sandstone tomb with an octagonal shape faces a charbagh and is considered a kind of precursor to the Taj Mahal. Its perfectly proportioned double dome in marble, introduced for the first time, reveals a Persian influence.

Shah Jahan's royal city was built further north facing the river Yamuna and his seat of power was the impressive Lal Qila or the Red Fort. Chiselled out of red sandstone, the entire complex comprised Moti Mahal, Rang Mahal, Sheesh Mahal and Khas Mahal, Diwan-i-am and Diwan-i-Khas with rows of beautiful cusped arches in marble, the Pearl Mosque, the hammams or lavish bathrooms and exquisitely laid-out gardens. The interiors embellished with silver and gold columns, painted and mirror-studded walls, gilded arches and carvings symbolize Shah Jahan's love for beauty and splendor. Jama Masjid, the perfectly proportioned and largest congregational mosque, opposite the Red Fort stands amidst the busy bylanes, *bazaars* and several monuments of Chandni Chowk. The Mughal architecture in Delhi reached its culmination with the Red Fort and Shahjahanabad, and Shah Jahan emerged as the undisputed greatest Mughal builder.

The Mughal edifices built in sandstone or marble, inspire awe and admiration because of their size, symmetry, grandeur and formal gardens while decorative features like lacy screens, cusped arches, pietra dura-inlay work add to their beauty and grace.

The foundation stone of the imperial capital of New Delhi designed on the concept of a geometrical grid with squares and circles radiating from the central axis of Raj Path was laid by King George on December 12, 1911. The focal point of the new capital was

…ne Rashtrapati Bhavan perched atop the scenic Raisina hill. As the official residence of …e President of India this splendid complex built with marble and sandstone consists …apartments, court rooms, courtyards and halls, especially the distinguished Durbar …all which is the venue of important ceremonies. The exotic Mughal Gardens provide …fascinating backdrop to the entire scenario. The impressive Secretariat buildings …mprising the North and South Block stand facing each other on either side of Rajpath. …ne circular-shaped colonnaded Parliament House lies in the north direction. A walk …ong the majestic Rajpath dotted with fountains, canals and lush-green lawns on either …de leading to the India Gate, provides a most spectacular view. Also known as the …I India War Memorial, the India Gate is shaped like a triumphal arch dedicated to the …dian soldiers killed in World War I.

The uniquely styled, circular-shaped, colonnaded Connaught Place has retained its …riginality and popularity as a commercial and shopping centre despite being drowned …a maze of skyscrapes in the area. The National Museum, The National Gallery of …odern Art, Cathedral Church of the Redemption, The Hyderabad House and The Teen …urti House are some of the other important buildings of the British era designed in …e Indo-Saracenic style, which is an excellent hybrid of European, Greek, Roman and …dian cultures.

A complete contrast to these stately buildings is the Jantar Mantar Observatory …uated on Parliament Street. Built by Raja Jai Singh II of Jaipur in 1719, this intriguing …sortment of six instruments helped in astronomical observations.

Luteyns' New Delhi was essentially conceived as an open city on classic lines to …flect the glory of the British Empire. As the capital of independent India, New Delhi …s also continued to grow at a hurried pace in all spheres. Amidst the frenzied building …tivity all around, a few monuments like the simple and serene Raj Ghat and other …emorials, the colourful Birla Temple, the Buddha Jayanti and Nehru Park and finally …e exquisitely designed lotus-shaped Bahai's House of Worship in south Delhi evoke …miration.

In Delhi, the vibrant city of the old and the new, the skyscrapers inch their way …ongside ancient ruins; there are palatial bungalows and thatched hutments; five-star …tels and roadside eateries; departmental stores and pavement shops; the BMWs and …e cycle rickshaws; air-conditioned educational institutions and tented schools; the …mparisons are endless. In fact, Delhi, the capital of the world's largest democracy, …nsists of both a New Delhi and an Old Delhi.

Delhi's population of more than ten million belongs to people of all castes and …ligions, so there is an interesting diversity of style and culture which extends to its …mate also.

It is a true cosmopolitan city, ever on the move, encouraging and absorbing new …eas. Something different or exciting happens every day, be it the frenzy of intense …litical activity, or a protest march. Life here can be difficult but never dull. People …nverge from all quarters to this land of opportunity, so it is becoming one of the most …ngested and polluted cities. Yet, there are parts of Delhi which have open spaces and …ts of greenery. Apart from its monumental heritage, Delhi is also known as a centre …art and culture.

While the rest of Delhi is expanding its burgeoning boundaries with satellite …wnships equipped with latest infrastructure, there is an integral part of Delhi where …ne seems to have stood still. A walk through the narrow, crowded by-lanes of Chandni …howk, Dariba Kalan and Khari Baoli take you back to the Mughal times.

A wonderful city of myriad expressions, it awaits the future eagerly and yet …eserves its ancient heritage. This eternal city, encompassing many old cities and also …mbolizing India in miniature, has enjoyed a long era of undiminished glory and will …ntinue to do so for all times.

Above: A colourful balloon mela in Delhi.
Middle: Pragati Maidan is a venue for year round exhibitions and fairs.
Top: Delhi's famous gardens are in full bloom during the spring season.

Above & facing page top: Qutb Minar, a victory tower of the first Islamic dynasty. The five storeyed Qutb Minar in red sandstone is decorated with geometric designs and koranic verses.

*ove: The fourth century iron pillar is an ancient metallurgical wonder. Above right: The interior of Iltutmish's tomb is beautifully
rved with geometric and calligraphic patterns.

Top : Humayun's mausoleum is the first mughal garden tomb. Above left : The Sheesh Gumbad in the picturesque Lodi Gardens. Above right : The dargah of the great Sufi Saint Sheikh Hazrat Nizamuddin Auliya.

op : The Purana Qila or Old Fort was the citadel of Emperor Humayun's city named Dinapanah and also Sheh Shah Suri's capital
hergarh. Above : Safdarjung was a minister of Emperor Ahmed Shah and his tomb built in 1753 is among the last of the mughal
arden tombs in Delhi.

Top : The Red Fort was the seat of power from emperor Shah Jahan to Bahadur Shah Jafar's rule. Today, it is the place from where the Indian Prime Minister unfurls the national flag on every Independence Day. Facing page top: Independence Day celebrations at the Red Fort.

Above: The Rang Mahal in Red Fort was decorated with silver and gold embellishments. Facing page left: Red Fort's Diwan-Khas once housed the legendary peacock throne. Facing page far left: The exquisitely carved marble throne canopy in Diwan-i-am, Red Fort.

Left & Top: The largest and also the grandest mosque in India, Jama Masjid can accommodate more than 20,000 worshippers at a time during festivals.
Above: Delhi's old city as seen from the minaret of Jama Masjid.

The historic Chandni Chowk symbolises the Delhi of yesterday.

The modern day skyscrapers of Connaught Place depict the Delhi of today.

The India Gate or the All India War Memorial is an arch commemorating the soldiers who died in world war I.
An eternal flame dedicated to the unknown soldier buns underneath the arch.

op & middle: The spectacular Republic Day celebrations on 26th January at Vijay Chowk every year are full of pomp and ageantry. Above: The illuminated Rashtrapati Bhawan and Secretariat buildings during the celebrations.

The magnificent 20th century Bahai Temple is built in the shape of blossoming lotus.

e Laxmi Narayan Temple also known as Birla Mandir is a place of worship for the Hindus.

Facing page: The Sikhs throng the holy Bangla Sahib Gurudwara to offer prayers and seek blessings.

Top: The calm and peaceful Raj Ghat is the Samadhi of Mahatma Gandhi, the father of the nation and a staunch believer in non-violence.

Left & above: Jantar Mantar is an astronomical observatory built by Sawai Jai Singh II of Jaipur in 1724.

Top : Colourful Rajasthani handicrafts sold on the pavements of Janpath attract many buyers. Above left : Khari Baoli in Chandni Chowk is famous for its genuine dry fruits. Above right : The road side stalls opposite the Red Fort offer tempting spicy savouries.

Rare and fascinating collections of Indian handicrafts are on display at the Craft Museum galleries in the Pragati Maidan complex. Above : The colonnaded shops of Connaught Place have a charm of their own.

The outskirts of the ever expanding Delhi are still surrounded by villages. A few glimpses of rural life in Delhi's villages.

The Taj Mahal looks like a jewel from top of the entrance gate.

AGRA

The earliest mention of Agra, like Delhi, is found in the Indian epic Mahabharata as Agrabana (Paradise) while another theory describes the city as Agragriha or one of the earliest homes of the Aryans. But, historical evidences date it back to only 500 years.

After Timurlane's invasion, a bruised and battered Delhi was the target of many nobles, but, finally, the Lodi dynasty was successful in capturing it. Sikandar Lodi decided to shift his capital from Delhi to Agra in order to have a better control over his empire.

Agra grew into an important cultural and commercial centre in 1500 AD. After Sikandar's death, his son Ibrahim Lodi lost the first Battle of Panipat in 1526 AD to Babur, an Afghan noble, who became the first Mughal monarch. He also paved the way for the rule of the Mughals in India. From the reign of Babur to that of Shah Jahan in a period spanning over 100 years, Agra became synonymous with the Mughals and witnessed a glorious era of immense wealth, unparalleled enterprise and artistic talent.

Babur, in his brief but eventful reign, built Rambagh, the first Persian Charbagh with symmetrical pathways, fountains and running water. His son Humayun, built a new capital city-Dinapanah in Delhi but his grandson Akbar, the greatest Mughal ruler, returned to Agra, to build the strong and robust Agra Fort for himself.

In 1570, he shifted base to Fatehpur Sikri, 40 km south west of Agra only to abandon for Lahore after 15 years. Akbar finally came back to Agra in 1599 and continued to rule from there till his death in 1605.

He was buried eight kilometres north of Agra at Sikandra, in a garden mausoleum. His son Jahangir continued to rule from Agra but his love for a life of pleasure made him spend most of his time in the idyllic Kashmir valley while his wife NurJahan managed the state affairs.

After a bloody war of succession, his son Shah Jahan ruled for 30 years, inheriting one of the richest empires of the world, with an overflowing treasury, rubies and diamonds including the famous Peacock Throne. He also encouraged and patronized merchants, jewelers, artisans, poets, musicians and artists during his reign. But his happiness was short lived, because in the fourth year of his reign, his beloved wife Mumtaz Mahal died, leaving him shattered and heartbroken.

Shah Jahan built the Taj Mahal, one of the greatest monuments of love, in her memory. Though he later moved to Delhi and built a new walled city called Shahjahanabad in 1648, his last years were spent in captivity in the Agra Fort where his son Aurangzeb imprisoned him after usurping his throne.

Aurangzeb was unpopular with his people because of his authoritarian ways. The Mughal empire slowly began to disintegrate and by 1711, Agra was an undefended hunting ground for the Jats, Rohillas, Marathas and at last, the British.

In 1835, Agra became the capital of the north western province under the British with Sir Charles Metcalfe as governor. The people of Agra took an active part in the Indian freedom movement and the city became an ideal hiding place for many revolutionary activities. In 1935, Agra was combined with Oudh to form the United Provinces which was renamed Uttar Pradesh after India became independent in 1947.

The majestic Agra Fort spans the history of three generations of the Mughal dynasty, from Akbar, Jahangir to finally Shah Jahan. As young Akbar's first important architectural venture, it became a successful model for the later Mughals while building forts.

The robust red sandstone edifice, said to have been constructed on the ruins of Badalgarh Fort of the Lodis from 1565 onwards, is crescent shaped with the longer sides adjacent to the river Yamuna and the other two facing the Agra city. With a circumference of about a mile-and-a-half, its 21 metre high double walls are fortified with bastions and guarded with a drawbridge over the deep moat. The main entrance is through the impressive Amar Singh Gate built by Akbar.

Above : Emperor Shah Jahan immortalised his love for his wife by building the Taj Mahal. Middle : Mumtaz Mahal to whom the incomparable Taj Mahal is dedicated. Top : Emperor Akbar is considered as the greatest of all mughal kings.

Above: The ninety nine names of Allah on Akbar's replica grave in Sikandra.
Middle: An exquisitely carved pillar at Fatehpur Sikri.
Top: The famous Musamman Burj in Agra Fort.

In contrast to its rough exterior, the huge complex comprises of beautiful palace courts, mosques and gardens. Of the 500 buildings constructed by Akbar, only a few like the fort walls and the Jahangiri Mahal survive. This impressive palace, earlier embellished with gold leaf and precious stones, depicts an interesting blend of Rajput and Mughal architecture. The well-preserved palace has a chamber and courtyards with brackets, oriel windows, carved motifs, arches and a marble pool in front, which was once filled with rose petals for the queen.

Shah Jahan's Khas Mahal or private palace in white marble had a river on one side and gardens, fountains and waterfalls on the other. Its painted ceilings and golden pavilions with ornamental facades depict his lavish style. Anguri Bagh, an intriguing Mughal garden lies in front of the palace. The exotic Sheesh Mahal or the palace of mirrors, has walls and ceilings embedded with small mirrors that would glow and twinkle like stars when a lamp was lit.

Musamman Burj, the double-storeyed octagonal tower has exquisite chambers decorated with floral pietra dura inlay and delicate marble lattice work. Shah Jahan spent the last eight years of his captivity here, gazing longingly at the Taj Mahal, which reminded him of his beloved Mumtaz Mahal. A flight of stairs above lead to Diwan-i-Khas or the hall of private audience, lavishly decorated with fine pietra-dura columns. It had two thrones in white marble and black slate on the terrace for the emperor to watch the proceedings below. The impressive Diwan-i-Am or the hall of public audience is an arcaded hall within a large courtyard.

The ultimate symbol of Mughal wealth, the fabled Peacock Throne encrusted with diamonds, sapphires and rubies, was installed here under a protective alcove also embellished with marble inlay, pietra-dura and precious gems. It is said that Shah Jahan arrived in regal splendor to the call of trumpets and drums to sit on the throne.

Nagina Masjid was built close to Diwan-i-Khas by Shah Jahan for the convenience of Mughal nobles, while the Moti Masjid is situated near Diwan-i-Am. This quiet place with marble interiors, exudes an air of peace and tranquility.

The Meena Bazar or the imperial shopping arcade, though closed for public now, is still remembered as the place where Shah Jahan first met the beautiful Arjumand Bano who later, came to be known as Mumtaz Mahal.

Though Shah Jahan contributed lavishly to the aesthetics and decorative trimmings of the Agra Fort, it is Akbar who is remembered as the monarch who built this impregnable citadel still unrivalled as an embodiment of power and glory.

Akbar had established himself as a great and powerful monarch with his empire expanding steadily over the years. He had everything he desired except an heir. So, he went to seek the blessings of a Sufi saint-Sheikh Salim Chisti-in a small village near Agra. The saint prophecised that he would be blessed with three sons in the near future.

Akbar's joy knew no bounds when his Hindu wife Jodha Bai gave birth to Salim, (later known as Jahangir). He decided to build a magnificent city, on a rocky ridge 37 kms west of Agra, as a mark of gratitude for the venerated saint in 1571 and shift his capital there.

This breathtaking, fortified Mughal capital, which was to be the cultural and commercial centre, while Agra remained a military strong hold, also paved the way for a secular culture among the people of this brilliant and far-sighted ruler.

Chiselled entirely from the red sandstone of the rocky ridge, this sprawling and airy complex comprising elegant palaces, mosques, pavilions, gardens and numerous other edifices put together randomly, are symbolic of the perfect synthesis of brilliant craftsmanship and architectural styles. Akbar's triumphant return from a battle in Gujarat led to the building of the Bulund Darwaza, a 54-metre high southern gateway of sandstone and marble with a long, steep flight of steps. The new capital city was appropriately named Fatehpur Sikri or the City of Victory.

Construction of Fatehpur Sikri began with the Jama Masjid which is also the largest and the highest building built according to Islamic prescriptions.

In complete contrast to this large congregational mosque is the single-storeyed, jewel-like marble tomb of the venerated saint Sheikh Salim Chisti. Entered through the Badshahi Darwaza, the square-shaped tomb, rests on a marble platform. The tombstone of the saint lies under a beautiful canopy made of ebony, brass, mother pearl and lapis lazuli. An enclosed corridor with exquisite lattice work on marble screens surrounds the central chamber. Thousands of devotees, especially childless couples belonging to different religions, throng the sacred place for blessings. They tie tiny threads on marble jalis and pray for the fulfillment of their wishes.

The Diwan-i-Am or the Hall of public audience close to the Badshahi Darwaza, is a large enclosed courtyard with colonnades and an elaborate pavilion from where Akbar dealt with the problems of his people. On the west, lies the imperial palace of the Daulat Khana its distinction lying in its typical Indian style embellishments like fancy brackets and carved, bell-shaped pedestals. The Diwan-i-Khas or the Hall of private audience which seems like a double-storeyed structure is actually a single, chamber with a high ceiling. Its dominant feature is an exceptionally beautiful red sandstone column in the centre of the room with long supporting branching brackets clustered around it to look like a crafted flower. The most intriguing edifice in the entire complex, however, is the five-storeyed Panch Mahal. The first two pavilions of the palace are almost equal while the third, fourth and fifth diminish in size gradually. The last one is open and provides a spectacular view of the historical city of Fatehpur Sikri. This was said to be a pleasure retreat for the royalty.

This captivating city which had such a profusion of architectural wealth, also prospered in the artistic, intellectual and religious spheres. Though Akbar himself was illiterate, he encouraged many eminent scholars, poets, artists and musicians; the Nine Gems of his court like Raja Birbal and Tansen being very famous. It was here that Akbar propagated his eclectic religion, Din-i-Ilahi. But this dream city remained his capital only for 15 years. It was either because of the water shortage or the escalating tension on the north-west frontiers of his massive empire, that Akbar had to abandon it and shift to Lahore.

Today more than 400 years and four decades after it was created, this epic in sandstone stands deserted and desolate; its ruins echoing the tales and fables of the life and times of one of the greatest monarchs of India.

Akbar's passion for building made him plan his own mausoleum. He finally selected a site eight kms on the outskirts of Agra named Sikandarabad, after Sikandar Lodi. But, after Akbar's death, his son Jahangir completed the tomb in 1613. The tomb exemplifies the unmistakable elegant style of the emperor it so proudly commemorates. The main entrance is through an imposing southern gateway of red sandstone with decorative inlay work in black, white and yellow marble, creating beautiful floral and geometric patterns and fine calligraphy of Koranic verses. The mausoleum at the centre of the Persian Charbagh can be reached from the gateways leading to wide pathways which divide the area into four quadrants. The main tomb is a bright red, five-tiered pyramidal structure quite reminiscent of Akbar's buildings in Fatehpur Sikri. This is a deviation from the conventional design and form of the usual single-storeyed square or octagonal-shaped tombs built during that period. The first floor is a podium of arches with a doorway decorated with inlay work. The next three storeys have earthy sandstone pavilions with a flat roof and no arches topped by an open terrace intricately designed with latticed marble screens. Each screen has arches with a panel inscribed with Persian couplets. In the centre lies the replica tomb of Akbar, carved out of a single block of white marble, embellished with floral motifs and inscriptions carrying the 99 names of Allah. It is said that initially the roof was covered with a canopy made of gold, silver, brocade and precious stones and the famous Kohinoor Diamond, which is now in possession of the British Government.

The real cenotaph, is in unostentatious and plain sandstone and lies protected inside a dimly-lit chamber which can be reached down through a sloping passage. Like all the monuments built by Akbar, Sikandra also demonstrates a fine synthesis of Hindu and Muslim architecture and also emphasises the change from Akbar's strong and resilient style to Jahangir's delicate and aesthetic technique.

Above : Elaborate relief work in marble is a distinguishing feature of the Radha Soami Temple in Dayal Bagh, Agra.
Middle : Brightly coloured tiles are arranged in a geometric pattern on the walls of the impressive Chini Ka Rauza near Rambagh, Agra.
Top : The decorative details on the walls of the mosque that lies besides the Taj Mahal.

Above: Agra is visited by also tourists throughout the year.
Middle: A typical saree shop in Agra.
Top: A sweets shop selling "Petha"- a speciality of Agra.

On the east bank of the river Yamuna, at a distance of about four kilometres to the north of the Taj Mahal is situated, in picturesque surroundings, the elegant marble tomb Nur Jahan's father and an important minister named Mirza Ghiyas Beg in Jahangir's court

He was bestowed with the title of Itimad-Ud-Daulah, meaning the pillar of the state This splendid garden tomb also lyrically described as a jewel box in marble was built by Nur Jahan in her father's memory in 1622. A rare combination of white marble, inlay and lattice work, coloured mosaic and precious stones, it marks a transition from the conventional red sandstone to the refined white marble.

Entered through an ornamental gateway, this 17th century tomb stands in the centre a Charbagh on a low platform with four attached octagonal minarets. This simple structure has been made extraordinary with magnificent decoration on every inch of its surface The dado levels of the marble walls have blue, yellow and green tiles forming intriguing geometrical patterns while the other sections have predominant themes of flowers and still-life. The use of pietra dura stone inlay with semi-precious stones like lapis lazuli, agate jasper and onyx was an innovative technique used for the first time. The presence perforated delicate marble screens carved from a single slab of marble provide a beautiful contrast to the inlay work.

The tombs of Nur Jahan's parents made from plain yellow marble lie in the centre the mortuary chamber. The niches in the walls of the chamber are embellished with painted floral bouquets, fruits, trees and paintings of flasks and goblets in a wide variety of colour The roof is also painstakingly painted with gilded stucco and stalactite. The upper pavilion containing the exquisitely-carved replica tombs has marble screens in place of walls and a unusual dome shaped like a canopy.

As one of the most spectacular monuments belonging to Jahangir's reign, the use marble and jewel like carvings make it a precursor to Taj Mahal. The evolution of Mughal architecture which began with the laying of Rambagh, a Persian charbagh by Babur, continued to blossom under Humayun, Akbar and Jahangir. It finally reached its zenith in a grandios garden tomb, the pure and perfect Taj Mahal, that till today defies an apt description. people all over the world, Taj Mahal symbolizes India. When the fifth Mughal emperor Shah Jahan built this timeless wonder of marble as a tribute to his wife, it was more than just art and architecture, it was a great eulogy to sublime love.

After Emperor Jahangir's death, Prince Khurram managed to claim the throne after lot of bloodshed and became Shah Jahan or the conqueror of the world in 1628. He had a colossal empire, immeasurable wealth and a loving companion in Mumtaz Mahal. happiness, however, was short lived because in 1631, Mumtaz Mahal, who was accompanying Shah Jahan on one of his military expeditions, developed complications and died while delivering her fourteenth child. A devastated Shah Jahan had only one mission left in life. had to fulfil his wife's last desire by constructing a monument peerless in both concept and beauty, which would symbolize their eternal love for each other.

It is believed that nearly 20,000 workers consisting of labourers, carpenters, craftsmen artists and engineers worked incessantly for almost 22 years (1631-1653) to bring the project to a fine fruition. A virtual city sprang up on the construction site which was a piece of vacant land near the curve of the river Yamuna below the Agra Fort. White marble w procured from Makrana in Rajasthan, sandstone from Fatehpur Sikri and a wide variety jewels, precious metals and stones like gold, silver, diamonds, emeralds, rubies and sapphir were obtained from China, Burma, Persia, Baghdad and Europe. Shah Jahan was extremel pleased with the final product which is said to have cost him approximately five millic rupees. Mumtaz Mahal's remains were shifted from its earlier tomb in a garden by the riverside to its final resting place inside the Taj Mahal in a simple ceremony. Shah Jahan w also buried alongside his wife in the same chamber in 1666.

The entrance to Taj Mahal is through an imposing red sandstone gateway beautiful inlaid with black and white marble calligraphy and motifs in floral and geometrical design As seen from the doorway, Taj appears soft and dreamlike in its breathtaking splendo

The meticulously-planned lush green garden laid out in the front is a Persian charbagh with trees, red sandstone pathways, water channels, fountains and a marble pond in the middle reflecting the Taj in all its glory. The blue skies provide a perfect backdrop to its mesmerizing white contours. This whole setting conjures up an image of paradise on earth. Two identical red sandstone structures, a mosque and a guest house stand at the end of the garden emphasizing the perfect symmetry and harmonious proportions of the Taj. The smooth marble veneer of the Taj is responsive to every change or shift in light so that it acquires a different look at different times of the day and during different seasons. The benign rays of the sun lend a soft purple hue to it at dawn which changes to a dazzling white during the harsh noon, appearing gloriously golden against the backdrop of the setting sun and divinely luminous on a moonlit night.

Beyond the garden, the Taj Mahal soars to a height of 74.21 metres, yet appears very delicate and fragile. This unusual octagonal tomb stands in the middle of a marble plinth. The four facades of the tomb are flanked by main arches which are followed by smaller arches. Also adding to the balance of the tomb are four tall and tapering three storeyed minarets. The crowning glory of the Taj is its ingeniously designed bulbous white double dome nestling amidst four marble cupolas which lie above the central octagon.

Directly under the sheltering dome is the main cenotaph chamber; the heart of the entire edifice. The tombstone of Mumtaz Mahal lies in the centre while that of Shah Jahan is on the right, both looking like a pair of jeweled caskets because of their exquisite floral inlay designs studded with tiny precious tones. Enclosed by octagonal screens carved out of single sheets of marble which are embellished with lacy filigree work and precious stones they display a fascinating interplay of light and sparkle into the softly-illuminated chamber. The actual cenotaphs, however, lie in a crypt directly below, inside a dark and silent chamber.

The facades of the Taj are also resplendent with the finest material of decorative art. Panels with splendid carved relief work, floral sprays framed with pietra dura and stone inlay borders and inlaid calligraphy in black marble with Koranic inscriptions give the monument a jewel-like beauty. The Taj Mahal is indeed a flawless gem, a timeless wonder and a never-ending source of inspiration to artists, poets and photographers and, above all, the last and the greatest architectural flowering of the Mughal period in Agra.

Agra has come a long way from the days when stories of the Mughal wealth and splendour surrounding its fairy-tale courts were famous across the seven seas. Today, it is like any other urban city of northern India, yet it is different because it retains its medieval essence. Its serpentine bylanes, old houses, markets teeming with people and goods, take you back into a different age. Walking along the streets of Agra, it is quite likely that you will come across small dimly-lit workshops where artisans claim to be descendants of ancestors who worked in the Mughal courts. Thousands of visitors from across the world come here every day to experience the marvels of the Mughal era and in particular, the pristine beauty of the Taj Mahal. Environmentalists are concerned about the possible hazardous effects of pollution on this marble wonder and are taking steps to preserve it for posterity.

The craft tradition of Agra includes marble inlay work, zardozi or the zari embroidery and carpet weaving.

In a city steeped in history and architectural grandeur, every carved pillar and embellished slab of marble is an affirmation of the consummate skill and brilliant workmanship of the artisans of that age. Each Hindu and Muslim king who ruled here, left a deep imprint on its cultural and artistic heritage. Craftsmen vie with one another to create exquisite items in marble and wood-inlay work, carving, carpet weaving, paintings, embroidery and leather work. While the crafts of Agra are a shoppers' delight, the tangy aroma of Mughlai cuisine being cooked in roadside *dhabas* and other restaurants and the sweet and salty savouries available in the shops are strongly reminiscent of the imperial flavor. The glorious days of Agra may long be over, but for the visitor, this historic dream-like city with a rich legacy of art and architecture shall always remain synonymous with magnificence and grandeur.

Top : The decorative details enhance the beauty of Taj during the clear light of the day. Above : The monsoon clouds add a sense of drama to the world famous monument.

Top: When seen from across the river Yamuna, the Taj acquires an entirely different perspective.
Above: On a misty winter morning, Taj Mahal appears somewhat illusionary.

Preceeding pages: All the four arched facades of the Taj are perfectly proportioned and exquisitely decorated. The subsidiary cupola provide a harmonious balance to the central dome. The tiny columns surmounting each facade of the Taj as seen against the red sandstone guest house.

he cenotaphs of Mumtaz Mahal and Shah Jahan look like a pair of bejewelled caskets enclosed in a delicately carved screen. The white arble of the graves is embellished with beautiful pietra dura inlay work and calligraphy.

An amazing range of marble inlay work and exquisite jali patterns on perforated screens can be seen on the inner and outer facades of the Taj Mahal.

...mi-precious stones like lapio lazuli, agate, carnelian and others were used to create the delicate flowers and curving vines in Taj's ...mbellishments.

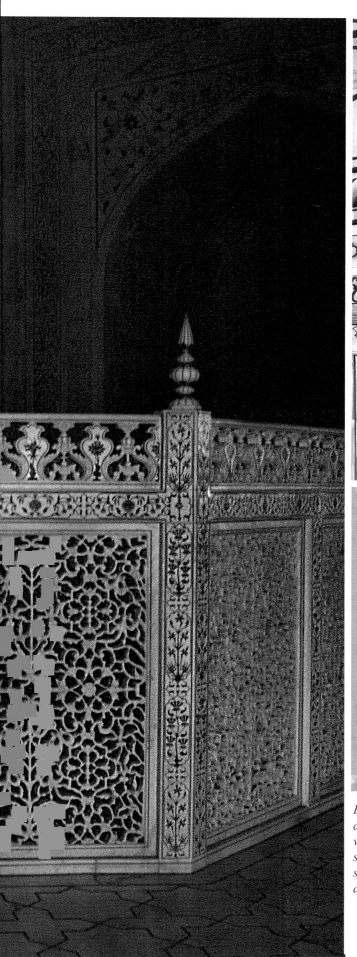

Each decorative design in the Taj has been executed with detailed precision. Perforated marble screens with intricate jali work have been carved from a single piece of marble. Floral sprays carved in relief on marble and sandstone enhance their surface texture. The predominant use of flower motif in the Taj decorations symbolises the garden of paradise theme.

Marble inlay, relief carving, jali and enamel work, painting, and calligraphy techniques have been used to beautify the Taj.

i Mahal symbolises India to people the world over.

*Facing page top: The massively proportioned
Agra Fort can only be entered through
Amar Singh Gate.*
*Facing page left & far left: The Water Gate and
The Darshani Gate at Agra Fort.*
Top: The double storeyed Machhi Bhavan.
*Left & above: The Jahangiri Mahal at
Agra Fort built by Akbar for his favourite
son has beautifully carved interiors.*

Top: The beautiful Moti Masjid or Pearl Mosque in Agra Fort stands facing the river Yamuna.
Above: The impressive Diwan-i-am in Agra Fort is built in Shah Jahan's characteristic style.

Top: The Golden Pavilion in the Khas Mahal, Agra Fort has lavishly decorated gold interiors.
Above: The Sheesh Mahal has exquisite glass mosaic decorations.

Top: The tomb of Itimad-ud-Daulah is often described as a 'jewel box in marble'. Above: Inlay panels in floral and geometric motif and delicate marble screens cover every inch of the exterior walls of both the floors.

The Itimad-ud-Daulah's tomb chamber is embellished with painted and gilded stucco and stalacite designs.

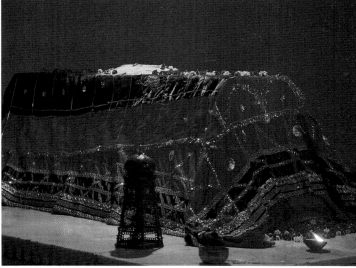

Facing page: The gateway of Akbar's tomb at Sikandra has dramatic inlay columns on its arches.

Top: The majestic four storeyed tomb of Akbar consists of red sandstone pavilions.

Left: The interior walls of Akbar's mausoleum are exquisitely embellished.

Above: The real tomb stone of Akbar rests below in a crypt inside a chamber.

An aerial view of Akbar's majestic mausoleum at Sikandra, on the outskirts of Agra city.

The Buland Darwaza, the largest gateway in the world, commemorates Akbar's victory over Gujarat.

A beautiful view of Akbar's imperial city at Fatehpur Sikri. The white marble shrine of venerated Saint Salim Chisti seems like a pea[l] *among the other red sandstone structures in the courtyard.*

ght above: Exquisite marble screens at Sheikh Salim Chisti's tomb.
o: Believers tie threads on the screens for fulfilment of their wish at the holy dargah.

Top: The exquisitely carved sandstone pillar at Diwan-i-Khas, Fatehpur Sikri. Above: The Diwan-i-Khas at Fatehpur Sikri appears be double storeyed but actually has a single floor.

op: A view of the historic Buland Darwaja from the inner courtyard of Fatehpur Sikri. Above: The Panch Mahal, an intriguing five oreyed structure has open pavilions.

Jaipur is a meticulously planned city.

JAIPUR

Unlike Delhi and Agra which were built steadily over the years by successive rulers, Jaipur is the culmination of a dream envisaged by a visionary Raja Jai Singh II. Even as an eleven year old prince, he had the courage to face the then Mughal emperor Aurangzeb, when summoned to a Delhi court. The authoritarian king caught hold of his arms and asked him, "Tell me, of what use are your arms now?" Totally unfazed, young Jai Singh replied, "When a bridegroom takes his bride's hands in his own during the wedding ceremony he vows to take care of her throughout his life. Similarly, with Your Majesty's long arms to protect me, what other arms do I need?" Impressed by the ready wit and spontaneous reply, Aurangzeb conferred upon him the hereditary title of Sawai (meaning one and a quarter more in worth than the others) and offered him lifelong support.

Sawai Jai Singh was the last of the illustrious kings of the Kachchwaha dynasty ruling over Amber from 12th century onwards. Claiming lineage from the sun, moon and stars, the Kachchwahas were migrants from Central India before consolidating their position in Amber which was earlier ruled by a Meena tribe.

Rajasthan or the land of Rajputana, as it was earlier known, is believed to be a very ancient civilization existing even before the Harappan culture. Though an arid desert land, few of its fertile areas came to be inhabited by certain tribes and nomads and these slowly grew into kingdoms constantly at loggerheads with one another. From this war-like ethos, emerged the martial race of the brave, loyal and chivalrous Rajputs who transformed the harsh and barren landscape into a land of golden sands and vivid colours. Each kingdom ruled by a raja or maharaja built its own fortified citadel for protection against the neighbouring enemy. After the advent of the Mughal rule, their struggle for survival intensified. While some kingdoms fought relentlessly against them, other clans chose the conciliatory middle path. The Kachchwaha dynasty who were always on good terms with the Mughals, further strengthened the bond when the mighty Akbar married the daughter of their chief Bihari Mal. His son too acquired an eminent position in the emperor's court while his grandson Man Singh became his most trusted general.

Sawai Jai Singh II became an influential administrative and diplomatic adviser during Aurangzeb's rule and this led to a dramatic increase in the strength and stature of Amber. The death of Aurangzeb was also the beginning of the decline of the Mughal empire, and an astute Jai Singh slowly withdrew from the scene to build a new city for himself which would earn him fame and also bear his name. The foundation stone of this well-planned beautiful city which was to be constructed from start to finish, was laid on November 25, 1727 below the protective environs of the Nahargarh fort towards the south of Amber. Jai Singh sought the services of a renowned Bengali scholar and engineer Vidyadhar Chakravarty, who meticulously planned the new city according to a simple grid system based on *Shilpa Shastra*, an ancient Hindu treatise on architecture. The ensuing six years saw an area of 50,000 sq km of waste land consisting of rugged ravines and forests, sandy dunes and sleepy villages being transformed into a spectacular fortified city which was to enjoy a privileged position in the history of Rajasthan.

Jai Singh II was an able and efficient ruler, but his death in 1743, led to a battle of succession and internal strife. The external disturbances from the growing influence of the Marathas and Jats also added to the woes. A disturbed Jaipur being ruled by Maharaja Jagat Singh and other states facing a similar threat signed a treaty with the British resident Sir Charles Metcalfe, whereby these states known collectively as Rajputana were to be supervised by the British, but the princes were allowed a hold on their states. After India became independent, Raja Man Singh II became *Rajpramukh* or the head of the newly-formed Rajasthan union.

Rajasthan was declared a state the following year and Jaipur became its administrative and commercial capital. Jaipur, a meticulously-planned urban city, consisted of seven blocks of buildings divided by very wide tree-lined avenues which were surrounded by

Above: The latticed windows and projecting balconies of the famous Hawa Mahal.
Middle: Sawai Jai Singh II, a visionary who built the city of his dreams Jaipur.
Top: Huge gates like this one mark the entrance to City Palace.

Above: The cannon at Jaigarh Fort is said to be the largest in the world.
Middle: The recently built Laxmi Narain Temple in Jaipur.
Top: Fine sculptural details from the Jagat Shiromani Temple at Amber.

a crenellated wall punctuated with seven gates. In this geometric plan, the straight and parallel roads were intersected by spacious *bazaars*, palaces and other important edifices. While laying importance on the meticulous design and symmetrical beauty of the city, Jai Singh's sharp and calculating mind thought of the commercial angle too. So he invited several craftsmen, artists and merchants to come and live in the new city thereby sowing the seeds of a rich legacy of craftsmanship and trade that thrives till today. Another important tradition still adhered to is that of people living in the walled city have to colour their houses in pink. This law was enforced by Maharaja Ram Singh when the Prince of Wales visited the city in 1876.

The nucleus of this Pink City, as it is now called, is the sprawling City Palace or Chandra Mahal covering almost one-seventh of Jaipur's area. The complex built in a delightful mix of Rajput and Mughal styles of architecture, can be entered through the Sirekh-ki-Deorhi gate on the eastern side leading to the outer court or Jaleb Chowk which also houses several other buildings like the Nakkar Khana or the drum house. In the centre of the courtyard lies the Mubarak Mahal, a two-storeyed marble building built by Madho Singh II in 1900. This beautiful palace has exquisitely-carved screens and scalloped arches on its exterior walls to give it a delicate appearance. Earlier functioning as a state secretariat and then as a guest house, today it is a textile museum displaying an exciting range of dresses worn by the royalty. The Sileh Khana in the north-west corner of the courtyard contains an awesome collection of traditional armoury which is among the finest in the country.

Two extraordinary marble elephants carved out of a single piece of marble standing at the gleaming entrance of Rajendra Pol are significant because they were gifted at the birth of erstwhile Maharaja Bhawani Singh. There was tremendous jubiliation because a male heir was born in the royal family after nearly a century. Beyond the gateway is the pillared courtyard of Diwan-i-Khas which was used during special occasions. Built on an open-arched plan, it houses two massive silver urns, each weighing more than 2,000 kilos and having a capacity to hold 1,800 gallons of water each. These were used to carry the holy *GangaJal* when Madho Singh II went to Britain in 1900, the first Kachchwaha ruler to do so. The famous Ridhi Sidhi Pol has a courtyard with four beautifully decorated gates depicting the moods of the peacock in exquisite frescoes. Close to it, lies the luxurious and opulent Chandra Mahal built by Jai Singh II with further additions made by successive rulers. The creamy-white ornamental palace has seven storeys, each floor having been decorated differently. One section of the magnificent palace is still the royal residence of the ex-Maharaja. On the other side of the palace complex lies the Diwan-i-Am, now converted into a museum exhibiting a rare collection of ancient manuscripts, portraits, palanquins, chandeliers, a golden throne and a fascinating range of priceless miniature paintings in the Rajput style.

To the north of Chandra Mahal lies the famous 18th century temple of Govind Devji, which enshrines the idol of Lord Krishna, the family deity of the Jaipur royalty. Also an integral part of the complex is the Hawa Mahal or the Palace of Winds, a landmark of Jaipur city. This odd pyramidical–shaped, five-storeyed structure was built by Maharaja Pratap Singh in 1799. The top three floors of this uniquely-designed building are just a room deep while the lower sections have connected rooms and courtyards. The tapering facade with 953 latticed windows, perforated screens and projecting balconies lend a delicate fringe to this airy structure which is actually the rear portion of the building. This tier-upon-tier composition was a platform for the royal ladies in *purdah* to watch the scenes of everyday life on the streets.

Sawai Jai Singh II's passion for astronomy led to a giant open-air observatory in 1734 known as Jantar Mantar. He consulted various scholars, acamedicians and astronomers for this ambitious project to make important observations of the position of stars, planets and measurement of time. In order to achieve accuracy, the instruments were made from stone and marble. The Samrat Yantra is a huge sundial to measure the distance, altitude and the diameter of the sun, while the Jai Prakash Yantra records the sun's journey through the sky. The Ram Yantra studies the movement of the stars whereas the Rashvalayas Yantra with 12 small sun-dials unravels the mysteries of the zodiac signs. Jai Singh set up similar observatories in Delhi, Ujjain, Varanasi and Mathura also.

The Albert Hall Museum in the Ram Niwas Garden was begun by Ram Singh II in 1876 to commemorate the visit of Prince Albert who also laid its foundation stone. Made out of marble and sandstone in the Indo-Saracenic style of architecture, it has a treasure of Indian, particularly Rajasthani arts and handicrafts, medieval brass plaques, Rajput armoury and sculptures, besides several other rare and distinguished items.

Jaipur's rich and royal heritage is also preserved in its various other splendid and opulent palaces like the Jal Mahal in Man Sagar lake, the Ram Bagh Palace which is now a hotel, the Moti Doongri Palace of Rajmata Gayatri Devi and Sisodia Rani ka Bagh and the Samode Palace on the outskirts of the city.

An 11-kilometre drive north of the busy and bustling Jaipur city on a narrow meandering road, takes you to a quaint little township dotted with old houses, small shops and a rambling stone structure. Suddenly a breathtaking sight of the forbidding exterior of the medieval fort of Amber emerges into view. Nestling below the protective visage of the Jaigarh Fort and cocooned amidst the ranges of stately Aravalli hills, the fortified palace and its sprawling walls are silhouetted against the natural contours of the terraced plateau. The entire picturesque setting is reflected in the clear, placid waters of the Maota Lake below.

Amber occupied a place of pride as the citadel of the Kachchwaha dynasty for nearly 600 years from 12th century onwards till Jai Singh II chose to abandon it for Jaipur, visiting it only during special celebrations.

The Kachchwahas had gained prominence during Emperor Akbar's reign, when he married their princess Jodha Bai, who later gave birth to Akbar's son and successor Jahangir. Akbar's policy of religious tolerance endeared him to everyone while his shrewd diplomacy in befriending the brave Rajputs added to his martial strength. The Kachchwahas in return gained power, prestige and prosperity. It was Akbar's trusted commander and confidant Raja Man Singh I who was responsible for creating most of the fortress palace, which was later completed by Raja Jai Singh I.

After a steep climb or a delightful elephant ride past the rugged ramparts and battlements, the entrance to the historic Amber Fort is through the ached gateway of Surajpol leading into the Jaleb Chowk or the grand square courtyard, now inhabited with shops. A few steps to the right lead to the beautifully carved silver doors of the sacred Shitla Devi Temple which enshrines the war-goddess Kali, the family deity of the Kachchwaha clan. The image in the form of a stone was brought by Raja Man Singh I from Bengal. The second courtyard takes us to the spectacular Diwan-i-Am built by Jai Singh I. This open pavilion with double row of marble and red sandstone pillars with finely carved elephant brackets, frescoes and latticed galleries speak of a strong Mughal influence. To the right is Ganesh Pol, a massive two-storeyed ceremonial gateway, exuberantly embellished with floral motifs, glass mosaics, frescoes, latticed stone galleries and a painting of Lord Ganesh (the god of learning and good fortune), which leads to the third court. Here, three private palace apartments are built around Aram Bagh, an ornamental Mughal garden. To the right is Sukh Niwas or the Hall of pleasure with ivory inlaid fragrant sandalwood doors. Its elaborate fountains and black and white marble chutes keep the interiors cool and refreshing.

Above and middle:
Elephant and Horse Polo
are still practiced in Jaipur.
Top: Women dressed in all their
finery ride the swings during
the monsoon festival of Teej.

At the other end of the garden is Jai Mandir, the private apartments of Jai Singh I, said to be the most exquisitely decorated of all Rajasthani palaces. Its walls and ceilings have carved marble panels embellished with silky smooth murals depicting flowers, motifs and war scenes. There are candles, deities, flowers even in the niches of the walls which are also studded with glass and sparkling precious stones. This perfect blending of the Hindu and Muslim styles, depicts the tremendous skill of the artisans. The Jai Mahal, on the ground floor, has scalloped arches decorated with flowers and butterflies and the exotic. Sheesh Mahal is embedded with mirrors that twinkle like a

Above: The colourful leather 'jooties' of Jaipur. Middle: The traditional block printing of Sanganer. Top: The ethnic mirror work embroidery is a household craft learnt by the women of Jaipur.

starlit sky when a candle flame is lit inside its closed doors.

The Jas Mandir close by, is famous for its glass inlay, alabaster relief work on its ceiling, latticed windows and very fine marble screens which bring in fresh breeze and also provide a panoramic view of Dilaram Bagh set amidst the Maota Lake. Narrow passages from the garden court lead to the fourth court surrounded by Raja Man Singh's palace and the *zenana* or the apartments for his twelve queens. These oldest buildings in the complex are characterized by their simplicity and Mughal architecture which can be seen in the covered balconies, screens and a colonnaded pavilion.

The Chand Pol, right opposite the Suraj Pol, leads to a pathway overlooking the Kadmi Palace, the earlier citadel of the Kachchwahas. Amidst the fragmented ruins here lie some crumbling palaces and mansions, broken and forgotten cenotaphs and places of worship, still in use, like the 15th century Narsimha temple, the famous Jagat Siromani temple built by Man Singh in the memory of his son and a Shiva temple of Ambikeshwara, from which the city is said to have derived its name.

With the passage of time, Amber may have lost its past glory, but combined with the myth and legends of its turbulent history, the palace still retains a magic and mystique all its own.

Nature has provided the people of this state who were earlier largely dependent on farming for their living with an arid desert land. Taming the harsh environment with their resilience and tenacity, they balance their hard lives by colouring it with vibrant colours, in the form of festivities and celebrations or expressing their creativity with the vast treasure of traditional arts and handicrafts. Deprived of natural colour, but bestowed with an inherent aesthetic taste, the people surround themselves with beautiful things. This craft tradition is so deeply entrenched in their lives and so intricately woven in their social tapestry that it runs like a common thread through the different sections of the society. Even the humblest of their dwellings are decorated with wall paintings, mirror work, mosaics and patchwork *torans*. They cook their food in burnished copper or terracotta utensils using carved spoons and ladles. The parched landscape is enlivened by a riot of greens, reds, yellows, pinks and blues in the *lehanga* or long skirts, *kurta* or blouse and *odhni* or veil worn by women and white *kurta pajama* with colourful turbans of the men. These colourful fabrics are either printed in dyes or embroidered and seldom worn plain. Sanganer and Bagru, the two towns on the outskirts of Jaipur, specialize in traditional block-printing textiles, wherein wooden blocks carved with floral and geometric patterns and symbolic motifs are dipped in vegetable colours made from extracts of flowers and minerals, and then hand printed and dried. In the evergreen *bandhini* or tie-and-dye work, the design is drawn on the bleached cloth which is tied with threads in small knots and then dyed in the required shades. The knotted parts, when opened, remain uncoloured. While *bandhini* is usually done in dots, circles and motifs, the *lehariya* design has diagonal stripes. Most of the rural women are trained in mirrorwork, patchwork and chain-stitch embroidery in a variety of hues and designs which are incorporated on textiles, tapestry and linen. The art of weaving wool or handloom on the pit loom inside the courtyard is a virtual cottage industry. This expertise is a Mughal influence and fabulous hand-knotted carpets and *durries*, at times, further beautified with *pattu* embroidery, are really sought after. Puppets and toys in cloth and wood earlier made to humour the village children, today find a place in urban homes as decorative items.

The famous artisans of Jaipur are also extremely skilled in carving brassware inlay on ebony and *sheshum* wood for furniture. The marble from the Makrana mines renowned for its usage in the Taj Mahal is quarried and shaped into religious idols, statues urns and other ornamental items. Leather or camel hide *mojris* (footwear) embroidered with thread, applique or beadwork are known for their comfort and elegance. The handmade paper from Sanganer is also much in demand all over the world.

While the fine stylized art of miniature painting seeped in through the Mughals, the brightly-coloured *phad* paintings and *pichwais* have a strong base in folk culture. The dexterity with which a village potter spins his wheel and creates the perfectly shaped matka or pot from a lump of mud with his magical fingers, is no less appreciated than the terracotta images of gods and animals carefully sculpted by them. While the terracotta is among the earliest craft traditions of Rajputana, the concept of blue pottery is confined only to Jaipur. This Persian art does not involve the use of clay but Fuller's earth which is mixed with sodium sulphate and crushed quartz to mould different items decorated with motifs in different shades of blue and green.

The Rajput women always attired in vibrant costumes are also never without their heavy chunky jewellery in bronze, silver or gold won according to their financial status. A *rakhri* for the forehead, *nath* for the nose, *paijeb* for the ankles along with a necklace, waistband and a large set of lac bangles worn almost all over the arm are among their favourite possessions. Exquisitely-crafted *kundan* jewellery embedded with gems and *meenakari* or intricate enamel work on different metals is a highly specialised technique that remains exclusive to the craftsmen of Jaipur.

The genesis of this rich craft tradition from a folk culture evolved with generations of a craftsman's family learning the skills through word of mouth and practical training. Later patronage from state rulers coupled with Mughal and other outside influences made it prosper and was ultimately sustained because of society's age old beliefs and customs.

This emphasis on faith and rituals till todays also gives them an opportunity to celebrate certain important religious, historical and seasonal occasions as fairs and festivals. A gay spirit fills the air as people dressed in traditional finery come together to offer prayers, eat, sing and dance rhythmically to their folk music with tremendous joy and cheer. While festivals like *Holi, Dussehra* and *Diwali* are celebrated with as much enthusiasm as in the rest of the country, the local festivals reflect an entirely distinct fervour and flavour. *Gangaur* is a fortnight-long spring festival dedicated to goddess Gauri, the consort of Lord *Shiva*, which culminates with her bedecked images being carried in a ceremonial procession. The Elephant Festival is celebrated in March on the day after Holi. Beautifully-decorated elephants are taken out in a procession and various competitions and games including the Elephant Polo are also organised. The *Chaksu* Fair is held on *Shitla Ashtami* in March every year and prayers and special food items are offered to Goddess *Shitla* to protect the people from smallpox. *Naag Panchami* celebrated in July/August is dedicated to snake deities who are said to have associations with Hindu gods and goddesses. During the monsoon festival of *Teej*, the women in *lahriya* clothes with their hands decorated with intricate *henna (mehndi)* designs, enjoy themselves on swings hung on trees and seek the blessings of Goddess *Parvati* for marital bliss.

These festivals bring the people closer to one another and in sync with their culture. This link enables the glorious past to flow into the effervescent present and also gives an insight into the distinct characteristics of the vibrant city.

Above: The blue pottery is said to have originated from Persia.
Middle: A potter at work on his simple wheel.
Top: The miniature paintings have a market all over the world.

Facing page top & below: The unusually designed five storeyed Hawa Mahal is the most photographed monument of Jaipur.
Top: The picturesque Jal Mahal appears to rise from the Man Sagar lake.
Left: The Albert Hall or the Central Museum in the Ram Niwas Garden.
Above: The famous Govind Devi Ji temple is a very important place of worship for the people of Jaipur.

Facing page & top: Maharaja Bhawani Singh doing shastra (weapons) pooja and performing religious rituals during the Dussehra festival. Above: Princess Diya Kumari is being greeted on her birthday.

Facing page top: The seven storeyed Chandra Mahal is extravagantly decorated.
Facing page below: The Diwan-i-Khas houses the silver urns, said to be the largest silver objects in the world.
Top: The Riddhi Sidhi Pol.
Left: One of the four exquisitely designed gates at Pritam Chowk inside the City Palace.

The Jantar Mantar is a famous open air observatory built by Maharaja Jai Singh II.

*om left to right: Chakra Yantra, Ram Yantra, Laghu Samrat Yantra, Narivalaya Yantra, Samrat Yantra, Rashivalaya Yantra and Jai
akash Yantra.*

Jaipur is a colourful kaleidoscope.

...spite a hard life, the people love to sing and dance.

Facing page: The women observe certain rituals during a folk festival while the men perform the Gair dance outside the Tripolia gate.
Top: A colourful procession during the Gangaur festival.
Left: The annual Chaksu fair near Jaipur.
Above: Ladies applying henna during the festival of Teej.

Facing page top: Some colourful cloth puppets.
Facing page far left: The famous Dhola-Maru folk painting.
Facing page Left: Fine mirror work embroidery.
Above top: A beautiful wall painting.
Left: The intricate art of weaving.
Above: The famous enamelled jewellery.
These are some of the famous crafts of Jaipur.

The majestic fort palace of Amber lies amidst the Aravalli ranges.
Left below: A view of the historic city of Amber from the Jaigarh fort.
Above: The steep climb to Amber fort can be enjoyed on elephant back.

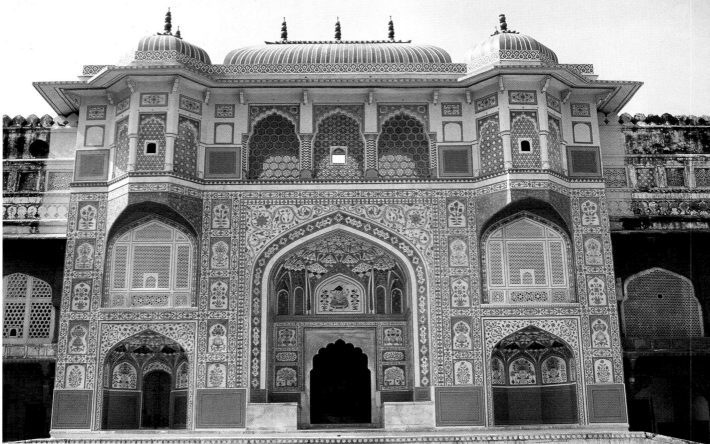

Above: Ganesh Pol is a ceremonial gate in the Amber complex. Top: The Sattais Katcheri near the Diwan-i-am.

The magnificent Sheesh Mahal is embedded with tiny mirrors that twinkle like stars when a candle is lit inside the chamber.

Facing page: The superbly crafted screen windows in the lavishly decorated Jas Mandir provide a fine view of the Maota Lake.
Top: The 17th century Jagat Shiromani temple in Amber.
Above: Tourists at the Amber Fort.

Facing page top: The splendid interiors of the Sunheri Kothi or the Golden Mansion in Tonk, a town situated ninety kilometers from Jaipur.

Facing page below: The medieval Palace of Samode with richly gilded interiors and murals lies about forty kilometers north of Jaipur.

Top: The annual camel fair at Pushkar is an important festival.

Left: The Dargah of Khwaja Moinuddin Chishti in Ajmer is an important holy pilgrim centre for Muslims in India.

This Edition Published by

 Frontline Books
Email: deepanfrontline@yahoo.com

First Published 2000
Published by R K Publications
© RK Publications
16th Edition
Email: rupinderkhullar@gmail.com
Photographs & Text © Rupinder & Reeta Khullar
Designed by: Anisha Singh
ISBN: 978-93-80625-11-9 Soft Cover (English)
ISBN: 978-93-80625-27-0 Hard Bound (English)
Available in English, French, German, Spanish, Italian, Russian, Japanese & Chinese languages.
Printed in India.